Dysfunctional Digressions

by

Bruce L. Marcoon

DORRANCE PUBLISHING CO., INC.
PITTSBURGH, PENNSYLVANIA 15222

ISBN # 0-8059-6758-3
Printed in the United States of America

First Printing

For information or to order additional books, please write:
Dorrance Publishing Co., Inc.
701 Smithfield Street
Third Floor
Pittsburgh, Pennsylvania 15222-3906
U.S.A.
1-800-788-7654
Or visit our web site and on-line catalog at www.dorrancepublishing.com

For my family, my mom,
and Brandy.

I wish to dedicate this book to my family, my mother, and our yellow Lab, Brandy. I'd like to thank my friends and colleagues who have in some way inspired, encouraged, or abetted this effort. Thanks also to a very large number of students, both present and past. Of major importance, I'd like to thank God for a meaningful life, and for making me, perhaps?, a "bit off the wall." I ask Him for continued blessings for my entire family, my friends, and my students. Special thanks for Rea Redifer for the cover art; Laird Bindrim for the author photo; and Tim Durning for the "milkbone" sketches.

"An echo is but the
lonely shadow of a sound."

BLM
4-27-04

P.S. I think it's time we added a new punctuation mark to the language. It should be simply "☺."

.

Contents

* = story

Poem for Brandy

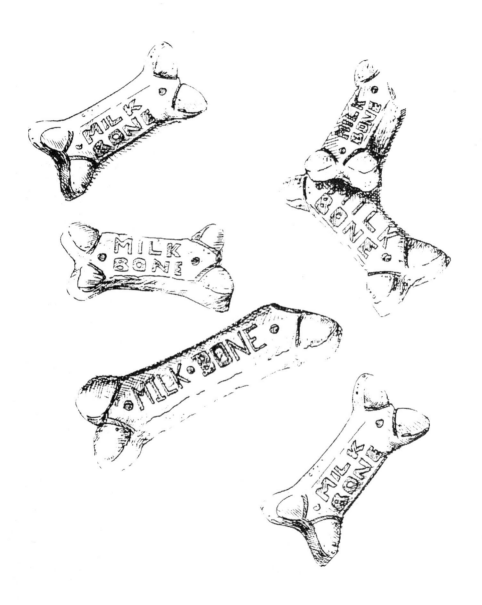

Illumination

Some of us are light.
Some of us are dark.
We all have various shades.
The great equalizer is the
Pure truth revealing light
Of the Sun.
When it shines on us,
We all cast shadows.

Between Today and Tomorrow

Time has forever intrigued me.
Within its grasp we can't be free.
It's artificial as measured by men.
Yet look how often we use the word "when."
We're taught to believe it's really the clock.
That that's not true may come as a shock
We take a concept which is really abstract
And treat it as though it were a fact.
It's said when having fun, time flies
Which makes our appearances seem like lies.
The countenance of a trouble being
Shows age and worry, that's what we're seeing
If time passes slowly when dealing with strife,
Shouldn't that slowness give us longer life?
Those who enjoy life - have fun in the sun
Often look older than those under the gun.
The problem of time is just a big mess
So it must not be real - that's my best guess.
Minutes and hours simplify what is deep
The real is a twilight zone much like sleep.
Then time is a falsehood, I must insist.
Perhaps that means we don't really exist.
       "I think, therefore I'm not."
       So much for Descartes.

A Reflection

Sometimes when you displease
or make someone ill at ease
the response is "go look in the mirror,"
which is to say take a good look
at yourself. Yet when you look in
the glass and raise your right hand,
the image raises the left. Isn't
that nice? What good is the advice
when the reflection is not you
but your opposite?

Sudsing Life Slimly

Life is like an automatic
Kenmore. There are various
cycles.
Born clean like a fresh garment,
you become soiled. Cleansing
needed, you go into an involuntary
program with dials turned by
someone in control.
First you are washed clean -
then you must soak to
figure it out.
Your mind is spinning so
it needs to be rinsed
for clarity. Then you
need to be spun again
for the final product, and
so it goes week to week
until you're worn out
and don't need to worry
about it anymore.
At any rate, it's
best to avoid permanent press.

See Me

I keep trying to impress you,
But you just don't seem to see.
I keep trying to entice you,
But you don't notice me.
I keep trying to amuse you.
You politely say "we'll see."
I keep trying to delight you,
But you're just ignoring me.
Why is it when I have to beat
The others off with clubs,
That when it comes to winning you
All I get are snubs?
Is it that you're taken,
Or are you just afraid
That if I am successful,
All you'll get is laid?
Or is it that you're scared
That I'm just teasing you?
Perhaps it's your protectiveness
That is misleading you.
I'm not the type for just one taste;
I wouldn't sink that low.
To be so cheap would be a waste
I want you to know
I'm searching now for the perfect way
To prove that I'm sincere.
I see you smile - you're going to play,
And now I'll hold you near.
I'll still try to impress you
Because I love you so.
I'll still try to delight you
So that your love will grow.

6

But you should be quite thankful
'Cause I was ready to give up.
Those who play too hard like stone
Sometimes end up alone.

Rewritten Love Song

I need to write another song.
 The last one got messed up.
The words were flowing right along,
 But the end was quite abrupt.
The first was written about her
 In different days gone by.
Then everything became a blur,
 I can't remember why.
Well, that was then, and this is now;
 No longer am I blue.
I was struggling, and then somehow
 I magically found you.
We were brave; we acted bold-
 Defeated our opposition.
It wasn't long- a band of gold
 Followed my proposition.
Still something was that wasn't right.
 Sometimes things just went badly.
You wouldn't quit without a fight.
 For that, I think back gladly.
You endured; you stayed in tune
 While time's toll mellowed me.
It's about time and none too soon,
 I sing my love with this melody.

Colors

I wonder if the
  spectrum is an infinite
Truth. Are there
words where light
  shining through
a prism could give
us hues for which
we have no words?
    If so, that's something
    I'd like to write about.

A Line

My love,
  You know I think
    you're the absolute.
Your loveliness transcends
    description.
Your eyes show the depth
    of your feelings
    and the beauty
      of your soul.
Your smile can warm the
          chilliest heart
Your hair softly cascades
        down
        like shimmering
          waterfall.
Your body entices,
        invites embrace.
It would be impossible
    to NOT
        love you.
I know you're reading these
inadequate words, and I imagine
how they please you—make
you feel good,
      BUT
my dear, you're so dense!
You've been ripped off—
you believe this junk!
Don't you know
      I say the same to
        ALL the girls?

Why Didn't You Tell Me?

Why didn't you tell me
    Before we made love?
        I sensed your sadness,
            But I didn't know why.
                Why didn't you tell me
                    You were going to die?

The Red Zone

Try to ignore it, but it's there—
a bad enough place to be when
it slowly oozes out from nowhere.
It's worse when it's sudden like
a flash of stark biting reality
shattering the softness of wishes.
Yet the iotas of pleasurable and
simple nice—those seemingly unable
to complete the why puzzle mollify
in the awareness that there is beauty
in sadness.

Words of Random Kindness

If you love a woman—really love her—
send her to get her nails done—and
maybe even a pedicure. After all, they
are such tactile creatures.

Afterwards, she can beautifully scratch
and stomp on your soul with pretty nails.

Junk Drawers

Everyone in a material
world needs a junk drawer,
with multiple objects having
forgotten histories—ideal for
browsing.
Some of the items are of use
and deserve better homes, yet
there is organization among confusion.
Many minds are like junk drawers.

Literary License?

I was going fifty—she
was doing ten when
she pulled out in a turn in
front of me. I crushed the
brake pedal and slid.
Angrily, I sped up with
correct intentions of loud
horn honking, appropriate
gestures and language—but—
when I saw the license
plate "DMBLOND" I couldn't
help smiling. I wonder how
much mileage she's gotten
from that.

Journeys

I came to Devon Prep
because strange travel
destinations are like "dancing
lessons from God."

To Be or Not to Be

The principal's office was cold and cheerless as I sat waiting for his return. It had the usual administrative properties: a brass nameplate "Mr. P.J. Johnson: Principal;" two framed diplomas, somewhat yellowed with age, from less than impressive colleges, and the compulsory family photograph complete with formal smiles. I looked at the son in hopes that he wouldn't turn out like the old man.

As I waited, I mused to myself, "So this is what it's like when a student gets his summons." Nervously, I shifted the position of my feet on the tan carpet. My boots needed polishing. "Oh well, I guess that's more ammunition for their side," I thought.

He came in briskly and closed the door behind him. Clearing his throat before speaking, he finally said sternly, "Pete, have you any idea why I called you down here?"

"No sir, but I'm sure you're gonna tell me," I replied, half lying.

"Well, Pete, you know that you have a reputation around this school as an outsider. By that I mean that you don't fit the mold. You're not a company man, not a team player."

"However," he continued, "on the other hand you're very respected. Your students achieve well, they like you, you're creative and you make people think."

"Yes, sir," I said, "I'm aware of all that."

"But," he responded, "rules are rules and you know that exceptions can't be made."

I looked at the pile of disciplinary referrals on the desk, very much aware that the same offenses did not always merit the same punishment. Real fairness was not part of the system of the school any more than in our legal system.

"Sir," I began, "with all due respect, this dress code is just another way of regimenting the faculty. If I have to rely on a 'uniform' to command respect and to do my job effectively, I might as well be a cop. You remember the TV show *Starsky and Hutch*. They were cops. They were excellent cops, and they didn't wear uniforms.

They were undercover cops. Maybe, I'd like to be an undercover teacher. A jacket and tie does not a better teacher make. Look, my boots and jeans cost more than that K-Mart suit you're wearing. Where do these crazy value systems come from?"

"Pete, you're missing my point. You no longer have a choice. It's a coat and tie tomorrow, no boots and jeans, or don't bother showing up for work."

"Sorry sir, maybe that's part of the problem. I don't see this as going to 'work.' 'Work' sounds like 'labor' or 'toil.' Teaching is a challenge and it can be tiring, but it's not as mundane as 'work.' Maybe, you're right; we want the students to conform. It's dangerous for them to think for themselves. I guess I'm a bad example."

"Pete, I don't enjoy giving this ultimatum."

"I know sir, but it doesn't matter. You, too, are the system. My mind is made up. I'll have my resignation on your desk by three o'clock."

"Pete," he said, "don't you think..." as I closed the door, breaking off his words.

After I had taken a few steps into the outer office, I remembered something else I had forgotten to say.

Retracing my departing steps, I knocked, opened the door, and poked my hand in.

"Oh, by the way, Dad, are Barb and I still invited for Sunday dinner?"

I thought back to the photograph on his desk. No, I wasn't worried anymore. I was okay.

Frustration 1

I'm boiling with RAGE.
I really want to hurt you—
    —to get back at you.
I want to insult you, but
    it's damn hopeless.
I can't seem to think of any
    insult simple enough
    for you to understand.

Bizarre

Wreaking
    mentallic
    twisting
            results
    in
    wrought irony.

Rent a Wreck

Is there someone who wants
    to rent a wreck?
I've been dented, smashed and
    ridden to the ground.
I still have some good parts left,
    but probably not for long,
The body is reasonably good—but
    only on the outside. In intense
    situation it performs fine—
    "purrs like a kitten."
You don't even have to pay a
    financial fee, and I guarantee
    mechanical performance—for a time.
    The only cost will be emotions;
    probably sadness, confusion, and
    frustration.
Like I said, I'm the product of
    many collisions. If you can
    use me, just let me know.
I don't cost all that much—so
    if you're tough—rent a cheapie.
After all, when my usefulness is over,
    you can just junk me. Someone
    else might want scrap mental.

Athena

Goddess of wisdom with gray eyes,
does their color affect your gaze?
Can you see through metallic lies,
or do you view through a misty haze?
What is this wisdom for which you're known.
creation of your father's mind?
At birth you sprang already grown.
Is it not through growth that we find
the abstractions, the truth, real life?
You, you were born wise, skipping the pain,
which as we stumble, cuts us like a knife.
Already having a superior brain,
Gray-eyed Athena, stare like steel,
if we were like you, what would be real?

Conversation Overheard at
Seafood Shanty (4-16-86) 8:30 P.M.

A yuppie couple sitting nearby...
I heard him say "A roll of film
Is like a bottle of wine."
The strange thing about this
Is I understood what he meant.

Seeking a Great Perhaps

I went to seek a great perhaps,
Without directions or even maps.
How far a journey even I don't know,
Or whether I travel too fast or too slow.
The goal of my search is a mystery
Which will be determined by history.
The quest provides both pain and pleasure
In qualities I'm not able to measure.
All I know is the trek is not over.
I'm simply destined to remain a rover,
Tasting all of what life has to offer,
Being neither an applauder or scoffer.
The guiding light, should I brighten or
dim it?
As I continue pushing fate to its limit?

Second Glances

Different types of second glances;
> Some from surprise; some from chances.
They're obvious or on the sly,
> Depending on the reason why.
A secret look is good advice
> When first observing someone nice.
At any rate, a second glance
> Can often spark a new romance.

Amusement Thought Ride

I was just thinking—I know that
in Disneyland or Disney World you
can spin in Alice's teacups. I
wonder then—if in Dollywood, you
can bounce in Dolly's "D" cups.

Epoxied in Time

Those poor lovers
on Keats' urn;
Their passion forever
frozen to burn.
Glazed too far apart
to nearly mesh.
Never, ever to
merge their flesh.
No chance for them
to feel life's range.
I'd have to find
that rather strange.
To be in such
a manner created,
would be too much.
I'd be very frustrated.
Then again, it
doesn't matter.
But still, that vase
I'd like to shatter.
Rather than just
to let them be,
I'd really like
to set them free.

Sneaky Poem

I'm sorry about your
       Christmas present. It's
       basically nothing. Believe
       me, no big deal.
I guess it's the thought that
       counts, mostly. They say
       good things come in small
       packages.
Besides, beauty, from my viewpoint,
       is in the eye of the beholder,
       and we have to think of
       basic necessities and maybe
       sometimes add a few frills.
Still, until you open the ribboned box,
       it must remain my secret.
That is—my secret and her's
       Oh yes—it's Victoria's Secret too.

King George's War I 1991-?

History will itself repeat
  And will never be complete.
An ugly ruler rears his head,
  And many people end up dead.
War is fought for power and money,
  And ego, too. Now that's not funny.
Uncalibrated rulers sit; slice their pie
  While young ones spill their blood and die.
Think about it; isn't it grand
  To die so young for grains of sand?
King George the Third we thought insane.
  Has Georgie Bush a better brain?

King George's War II 2003-?

History will itself repeat
    And will never be complete.
An ugly ruler rears his head,
    And many people end up dead.
War is fought for power and money,
    And ego, too. Now that's not funny.
Uncalibrated rulers sit; slice their pie
    While young ones spill their blood and die.
Think about it; isn't it grand
    To die so young for grains of sand?
King George the Third we thought insane.
    Has Georgie Bush a better brain?

It's a Sin

It was a real sin, an honest
      to God shame.
She was a wonderful woman, young
      alive, but, nevertheless, alone.
Her life was a cinematic single feature
      done in solo, a soliloquy.
The bottom line was that she was
      so ugly. The only love
letters she ever got were
      written in Braille.

One Final Lesson

It hadn't been a typical day at work; nor a usual week for that matter. The weather was starting to turn cold with a tinge of the gray iciness that heralded the approach of winter. Physically and mentally the absence of sunlight caused depression, and Friday turned out to be a disaster. Calamities like this were generally common in the teaching profession, but luckily for me, they were usually separated by a period of years.

Such confrontations with students had always been rare but had become non-existent. After twenty-three years dealing daily with adolescents in the classroom, I'd become a master at psychological dominance. I hadn't raised my voice at my students in over fifteen years.

Overall, I was respected and generally well liked, and I reciprocated with my feelings. But, that once in a while episode, when it occurred, was too much. Direct defiance did not sit well with me; it took me off guard and confused me to the point of mental fracture.

As the bell sounded the beginning of the second class period, I noticed a cluster of boys in the hall who were more than reluctant to enter their room next door to mine. Stepping into the hallway, I said, maybe with a bit of volume, but certainly not a shout, "Get in the room." Surprised faces slowly obeyed, except for one, who just grinned at me and shook his hands in mock terror. Almost losing it, I stepped close to him, purposely invading his space, and peered down. The runt was all of five-seven and maybe weighed about one-thirty, yet I hoped desperately that he'd take a swing at me. Eternal seconds of silence passed as glares were exchanged.

"You have a really bad attitude problem," I challenged.

"What are you going to do about it?" he dared.

"Just get the hell in the room," I snarled, my mouth feeling foamy.

The brat moved by me and swaggered across the room to his seat, looking back with cursing eyes while I boiled.

"On second thought," I said, "come here."

"Oh, where are we going?" he quipped.

"I'm not going anywhere, but you're going to the office," I mumbled disappointedly. The words were so wimpish. As I uttered them, they strangled my testicles. I knew he'd get administrative wrist slap if that.

"Oh, okay," he replied, smiling in his knowledge that my assessment of his punishment was true.

It's difficult to explain my feelings at that point. I felt he was a murderer about to be punished for jay walking. I know I suppressed enough violent energy to illuminate half a city.

The rest of the day went smoothly enough although a portion was spent talking to myself. Despite attempts to calm myself from the voices in my head, I was really frazzled.

Things like this just didn't happen to me. It took one snotty little bastard, too ignorant to know my reputation, which besides respect also carried the message "he's a great guy, but don't screw with him," to threaten the smooth running machine developed over a score of years.

Later in the day, I realized that although I'd seen the little ass in the halls, I didn't even know his name. Intuitively, I needed that information so I inquired of Mrs. Robinson, next door. The name was Chris Sanders.

That night at home the memory of the encounter still plagued me.

"Oh well," I mused. "It'll probably take a couple of days and then will pass into other such distant histories."

The weekend came and went, and the entire event finally moved to my mental recesses, but Monday morning on my half-hour drive to school the monster resurfaced. My classes went fine, were even enjoyable, but twice during the day I saw Chris in the halls. On the second occasion, he had a pretty young girl, an honor student by reputation, in tears. I ached to interfere, but thought better of getting involved in a teen romantic situation and settled for a patented stare vicious enough to disintegrate the little creep. He looked away. Then, I realized that it hadn't gone away at all; it was really getting to me.

I reflected back on my career. There had been a few times years ago when I'd snapped. Back when my images, from both self and student point of view, were not firmly set, students would occasionally take me for a test ride. A few times I had lashed out with a hand, or once even a fist when I was breaking up a fight. I thought about this in general as it related to the teaching profession.

The reality was frustrating. Once again, I realized that even in a small, docile school like mine, there was no authoritative control available. Corporal punishment had vanished decades ago, and at least two of my colleagues had lost jobs for such violations. But that wasn't the answer anyhow. Intellectually, I saw no need to beat up on students, even if they deserved it. My district, like many, was paranoid about a lawsuit-happy community, not only in matters of corporal punishment, but in almost everything. Expulsions were almost non-existent; so most troublemakers were simply put up with and carried along socially. All of this contributed to the other factors causing the educational impotence of the public school system. It wasn't that I didn't care, but I had frequently thought about what made kids like Chris the way they were. My conclusion was the legal system. God, how I hated lawyers and their whole negative influence on societal behavior.

Pressures eased as the day progressed, and Monday night Barb and I watched the Eagles whip the Cowboys, and I didn't consciously recognize the problem at all. I slept well, but Tuesday morning in the car, started thinking again—this time to the point of a headache.

Before second period, I saw Chris. This time it appeared that a tiny packet was quickly changing from someone else's hand to his, then to his pocket. He saw my glare and sheepishly looked away.

"Was it or not?" I wondered. Drugs wouldn't surprise me. It would be great to see him busted, but something told me to keep mum. No scenes, no undue attention. Chris was becoming an obsession. The bell rang. I wanted to trip him as he went into his room. That might piss him off. Maybe he'd take that swing. Then I could demonically demolish him and teach him a lesson. "No," I thought, "that would be too obvious."

I hung around late Tuesday, rather unusual for me, grading American Literature research papers. Soon it was later than I thought. While leaving through dim hallways, I noticed that the Guidance office was closed and unlit. Dazedly, I found myself using my room key which somehow had many more uses than intended, and let myself into the restricted domain.

Entering the tenth grade counselor's office, I flicked on the desk lamp and went immediately to her filing cabinet. Placing Chris Sander's file on the desk, I sat down and opened it. From the information confidentially contained, I realized that I shouldn't have taken his defiance personally. There was a significant history of problems. Broken home... poor kid... father an outlaw biker in jail in Pittsburgh... poor kid... forced to leave previous school... poor kid... semi-literate... poor kid... substance abuse... poor kid... poor kid... poor kid... poor kid...bullshit!

Reading on, instead of gaining more sympathy, I became angrier. With all the strikes against him, his life was destined to be a tragedy. Programs and institutions wouldn't work. It pained me to see the resources lavished on a few dozen scum in the system in vain hopes of rehabilitation, while greater measures of "good" kids with their own minor problems were neglected and had to fend for themselves.

Feeling no sympathy, I thought, "How many chances is someone supposed to get?" I suddenly stood up, replacing the file after making a few mental notes. Like a shadow, I made my way to my Jeep, almost knocking over a trashcan in the darkness. I guess I was a clumsy shadow. "Funny," I thought, "In more ways than one society had problems with trash. Chris was just another type of waste, irritating human excrement, which needed to be flushed."

I drove away listening to a talk show on the ride home. I wasn't in the mood for music. Barb had a special dinner that night, since she had to leave on a two day buying trip in Manhattan the following morning. That meant I'd have to buy my meals since I couldn't be bothered with cooking. I really didn't like that aspect of her job. I hated eating alone, and I missed her being at home when her job took her on the road. After dinner, I helped clean up. We talked a bit, watched a little TV, and then to bed.

Wednesday morning came too soon. I said goodbye to Barb and left in the rain for school. As I was driving, I was trying to decide what to get for dinner. I couldn't decide, but then again, dinner was a distance away, and food didn't fascinate me anyway.

The day was easy. The kids all had tests so I had little talking to do. After lunch, standing in the hall outside my room, I overheard a conversation. Three girls were talking about Chris and his girlfriend Becky. Apparently she was pregnant and he was demanding that she get an abortion because he was now involved with someone else. I shook my head in disgust. There he goes again. Takes a pretty girl with all kinds of ability, screws up her life, then dumps her. Yeah, that's what he would do, screw up his life and that of everyone in close contact. There really wasn't much justice in the world. Not much.

Near the day's end as I was walking to the office, I passed the creep once more. He had his new honey pressed up against his locker. Their lips were locked and his hands were traveling. As I drew closer, he ended the clinch, and as I was walking past, I heard the muffled word "asshole." I turned to look back to face a grin on his face. It wasn't said directly, just overheard, so I ignored it. It wasn't easy. I wanted to change that wise ass grin into a challenge for a cosmetic surgeon, but, with difficulty, resisted the impulse.

About two hours later, I entered my driveway, pushed the garage door opener, parked the car, grabbed my briefcase, and went into the kitchen. On the other side of the door Ashley loyally waited with a toy in her mouth - her usual greeting. Her tail circled like an aircraft propeller. I sat the briefcase on the kitchen table, and patting Ashley on her snout, noticed the "I love you" note from Barb. "Damn!" I thought. I'd forgotten about her trip. I felt lonely already. I hated those nights. I grabbed the leash and took Ashley for a good walk, a treat for her since we had an invisible fence and she seldom got to tour the neighborhood. Besides I was bored and restless.

As we turned down the street, I noticed the usual evidence of all the dog owners in our rural neighborhood. From a distance of two to numerous feet from the street onto the curbless lawns, according to the lengths of the various leashes, was a sporadic trail of dog crap. Ashley soon made her deposit, and we returned home. The recent visions brought Chris back to mind.

Well, since Barb was gone, I had to go out to grab some sort of dinner, even though I wasn't very hungry and I really didn't want to go out. Then again, I didn't feel like staying in the house alone. "Where to go?" I pondered. Suddenly, impulsively, I bolted up the stairs to our room. Quickly washing up and changing clothes, I checked a dresser drawer for money since earlier I had forgotten to cash a check. I was in luck. Looking in the drawer, I took exactly what I needed including enough to munch out and gulp a few beers. I ran down the steps and made a deposit in my briefcase which I returned to the car...so I wouldn't forget it in the morning Suddenly, I felt some energy—an excitement. I said goodbye to Ashley and headed for the Chadds Ford Tavern for that bite to eat.

It was about six o'clock and getting dark when I got there. Nancy was there as usual, tending bar and keeping the guys in line. I ordered a roast beef sandwich and a Budweiser and shot the bull with a couple of bar buddies.

A couple of beers and a contented stomach later, I said my farewells and plopped into the Jeep. Again, I felt restless, and there was no reason to go home. I wasn't tired, so I decided to go for a ride, although an inner voice told me not to. Hey, maybe I'd stop to see how Mike was doing. I hadn't talked to him in a while.

About twenty-five minutes later I was back in the area of my school and Mike's Bar. It seemed like I'd just left. As I neared Mike's, I noticed the street sign reading Grayson Street. Funny, I'd never really noticed that sign before, even though I'd passed it thousands of times. Downshifting into second, I slowly swung around the corner. Casually, I cruised down the street. There it was, number 402, the Sanders house. I was surprised. The place looked quite respectable from the outside. It was just that there was a plumbing problem. The sewer pipes weren't effective. I drove by slowly and continued for a couple of blocks.

Making a left, I headed back toward Mike's Bar. I passed a stretch of about two blocks parallel to the train tracks where there were no houses, only woods between the street and the tracks. As homes appeared, I saw the sign "Dante's Pizza." That was the local hangout for the high school kids. Staring through the plate glass window as I went by, I saw a group of kids around what appeared to be a video game.

There, on the edge of the gathering, he was. I checked out the sky. No light at all. The darkness felt good. I hurried to Mike's where I parked the Jeep in the lot.

Opening the briefcase once again, I took what I needed, that inner voice guiding me, but didn't go right into Mike's. Silently, like an Indian scout, I hurried back to those railroad tracks and followed them until I could make out Dante's in the distance across the street. Halfway between the pizza place and Grayson Street I hid in the brush. The timing was perfect. I didn't have to wait long at all. It was only about ten minutes until I saw Chris making his way home. At the same instant, I heard the 8:30 freight in the distance. The voice chuckled—he was alone, and totally unaware as I scurried up behind him, quickly fitting the barrel into the hole in the oil filter.

Then I was ten feet behind him, I yelled, somewhat drowned out by the approaching freight train, "Yo Punk." As he turned his ashen face, I saw the incomprehension in his stupid eyes. I smiled and said, "Well, Chris, I guess this is your final lesson."

The Smith and Wesson thirty eight barked quietly, but violently caressed my hand. As quickly as it had begun, it was over. Within three minutes, I calmly entered Mike's.

"Hi Mike! Howsa bout a Bud, Buddy?"

The cold beer sank smoothly as I smiled and started a conversation with Mike. Between words, I reflected. I asked that inner voice, "When will they ever learn? Will there have to be a number four, a number five....?"

Miss-Remembrance

I can't figure out
    why she rates this poem.
She sure wasn't much to look at—
    even somewhat on minus side.
No, she wasn't even pretty, and her body
    wasn't made for second glances.
More like you'd just never notice—
    sort of nondescript.
Come to think of it, she had a
    terrible personality to top it off.
Oh, now I remember—
    she had nice teeth.

This One's about You

Ya know, I don't want you
        to take this wrong.
This isn't any flirtation
        or love expression as such.
Not even a reasonable
        facsimile thereof.
It's just a subobjective
        portrait representing you,
And your various parts
        and their ways.
Glossy manelike tresses shine
        consistent like your smile.
A flash of upturned lips with
        ultra-porcelain blinds like
A photographer's bulb and could
        melt lead.
Somehow, there is a unique
        hardsoftness that portrays past pain,
Still remembered, but surfacely
        camouflaged by your warmth.
The tinted twinkle of your eyes
        paints mischief with zesty
Bubbles splashing onto those nearby.
        In short, you should be
Both embarrassed and ashamed.
        To be so beautiful is sinful.

Incongruity

One car with three
Rear bumper stickers:
"South of the Border,"
"Jesus Loves You," and "Go
Ahead Hit Me: I Need the Money."
Something doesn't seem right
About that yellow Chevy.

I Really Thought...

I actually thought it was meant to be.
There was so much in common—almost
too good to be true. Your strengths
were my weaknesses and mine were
yours. We completed each other like
the final pieces of a jig-saw puzzle,
and then you had to ruin it,
You went and burned the damned toast!

Hanging Ten in a New Millennium

Until a decade ago, I thought a menu
was something you ordered
a tasty meal from.
Forget about programmed misinformation.
I guess I'll just have to starve.

Global Warmth

When we wed, I
     promised her the world
     within five years.
On our fifth anniversary,
     I gave her an illuminated
     spinning globe.
She hugged me and
     rekindled mankind.

Frustration 2

I'm trying to write a poem
about all the things I've forgotten,
but I just can't seem to get very far.

Her Legs

Her legs look beautiful up
to the hemline of her skirt.
That's about as far as I can
go with this one.

Meltdown Dream

I had a
meltdown dream last
night—sort of Fellini-esque
    faces of
      friends amorphously
melting into other identities
    and back. It made
me realize how much diverse
    individuals have certain
    common traits.

Private Joke

Something funny just
happened in my mind.
I'm laughing inside. It's
very pleasant. I just
observed something that
made me think of something
else. It's going to
make me smile every time
I think about it today.
It's so neat, that I'm
going to keep it to
myself.

Aerosol Cans

Pressurized metallic
    cylinders. Depending
    upon content, one
    push on the button
    can be mystifying.

Whispers

Whispers are a paradox,
usually expressing
something of significance
insignificantly.

Ode to Beer

Frosted mug sitting before me,
      I wonder how you'll taste today.
At first cold, you're often refreshing
      but as you warm, you can be depressing
Sometimes appearing in bottles of brown,
      green usually better becomes you.
Either hides your true hue like urine.
      Your color and odor belie your taste,
ranging from bitter to slightly sweet—
      like life.
      What are we trying to quench?
Is it thirst, or bothered brain?
      Do your suds really wash away
bad memories, or do they create more?
      Perhaps your final double-vision
is both.

Schizophrenia

Nature is in her full glory
as I gaze out from the windows.
The flora are in full bloom and
the fauna are singing and running
mimicking mirth, but the blackness
will inevitably descend to blight
out that which is good! Torrents
will fall with thunder and
fire.
   Ah, the gentle breeze soothes, but
the damned warm waft will make me
sneeze.

Preverbal Poem

That's Amoré?

Scientists have claimed that
        physical attraction and
        subsequent love are
        chemically caused electro-
        magnetic phenomena.
Kirlian photography has provided proof.
        we can see the little charges
        captivating and intermingling—
        sexy little devils.
Don't despair. It makes little
        difference. I guess it's
        just love instead of
        "I love you forever," now
        I'll have to say—
        "Baby, these ions are
        for eons."

Light Plays

Bright lights plays with me all the time
In through my eyes and to my mind
I wonder if then when I blink
It somehow alters how I think
Mysteries which need detection
All caused by a small reflection
But now before my thoughts grow deep
I know there's no light when I sleep
So then about these words I've wrought
They just portray a scrambled thought.

Little Patti Pothead

Patti was a nineteen-year-old somewhat wilted child of the sixties in 1972 with visions of wisdom beyond her years. Her back to nature concerns caused her to wear minimal clothing and to idolize Johnny Appleseed. The former caused her to be constantly stared at since she had a body that even an abstract painting could not disguise and widespread popularity. The latter eventually caused her widespread popularity and not a little trouble with the law.

She was so enamoured with Johnny's legend that she bought a large book of U.S. maps to plan her life's work. I hesitate to use the word "Atlas" because it was much more appropriate in Mythical times. The modern world has changed from that globe shouldered by Atlas. Little countries and pieces of earth are falling off. Today, in addition to holding it, someone would have to weld it together. Perhaps his brother Prometheus, who gave us fire, should hold it and weld it at the same time. But certainly not the other brother whose little bitch wife Pandora opened her box and released all our troubles upon us. Yeah, that was some can of worms. Hell, they even got into the apples, but that's another story.

It just so happens that Patti bought her map book with scattered thought in mind. One day soon after her purchase she went back to her school, Tome Street Elementary, the only one she could remember. Her high school had disappeared into that rolled up fog that had enveloped her world for the past five years and was not readily available. So she returned to the library to seek that book on Johnny Appleseed that she had read twelve years previously as a bright little blue-eyed blonde of seven. The influence of that book must have been enormous to have remained in her memory, which at this point was in direct proportion to her functional brain cells. Ironically, that illustrated book portrayed Johnny as wearing a tin pot for a hat. Perhaps this is when it was determined that she should be a pothead too.

Yet, she knew she had to do research, as she called it, to prepare her life's journey. When she found the book, still in remarkably good condition, she found herself too distracted by the illustrations to concentrate on the words, and there were no maps indicating specific routes Johnny had taken.

"Well," she thought, "perhaps he just kind of wandered." Then she began to think, "How far could he have really gone? After all, how many apple seeds could one carry, and how did one come by that many seeds to begin with?"

Little did Patti realize that besides spreading orchards from the Pennsylvania western frontier in 1797, to Allen County, Indiana, where John Chapman died in 1845, Johnny also was sewing the seeds of something else within the new frontier. Johnny was also a Swedenborgian missionary preaching a new Christianity to be spread over the earth. Patti would have been incapable of seeing the inconsistency of his making apples available to his intended converts being that apples are the forbidden fruit causing deformities in men's necks caused by women's being pains in the same areas. It is also significant that a mass women's movement was but in its infancy then, having recently left the embryonic stage.

Patti, as you can see, was not a candidate for Mensa, but that was okay, she had no need to be, considering her exquisite beauty which she gave freely to many people. It's not that she was a tramp. She was mentally virginal. She just got very caught up in that timely saying, "If it feels good—do it." So she did, sharing her pleasure with legions of other free spirits and those who pretended to be— just to get next to her.

At any rate, Patti was determined to get on with her plan which was to spread happiness freely from Southeastern Pennsylvania as far west as she could, hopefully all the way to hippie heaven, San Francisco. As might be guessed, her happiness was largely artificially induced by marijuana. That's right—pot. Patti's scheme was to hike cross county as her hero had done some

170 years earlier, planting cannabis plants to euphorically please the masses. A modern approach to an apple a day, in her mind.

With minimal gear, she set off from Delaware County, Pennsylvania scattering her seeds carefully as she trod. At the end of the first day she had made it into Chester County where she camped out on the Brandywine Battlefield at night with other ghostly revolutionaries. Arriving in Kennett Square early the next morning, she passed an auto-body shop rife with an aroma that was not early morning coffee brewing. Here she made a deal with the proprietor—sex for seeds, and continued on her journey.

A few ride hitches later, she was amid the lush Amish farmlands of Lancaster County, and the home of SHOO FLY PIE. Walking along Rt. 841 to Strasburg, she was eyed suspiciously as an outsider by the Plain Folk who observed her. She thought they looked strange too. She certainly formed a contrast to their modesty. From her perspective the Amish women simply looked like inverted flowers.

Things went pretty smoothly considered that crossing Pennsylvania was very hard on her sandaled feet. The June weather was welcoming and it rained little, but by the time she reached Harrisburg, her pot seeds ran out. A few days in Harrisburg, using her God-given talents, replenished her seeds twofold. Indeed, she became a legend in seventy-two hours. She also was able to bathe in the Susquehanna before continuing. At times her back pack and sleeping roll got heavy and irritating, but a quick joint enabled her to see the humor of her situation.

Travelling parallel to the Turnpike she occasionally accepted rides by more than willing truckers who with hawk-like eyes had observed her bouncing along on well-tanned legs. Of course, she never stayed on board for long because when it was over she had work to do.

At last, after just three days on the road, she arrived in that soot mecca, Pittsburgh, again needing replenishment and refueling.

Tired and dirty, she arrived at the campus of Pitt. She caused quite a stir as she strolled along Forbes Avenue. On a street corner across from Bimbo's Pizza she encountered a few Hari Krishnas.

They were whooping it up on the corner like a group of Plains Indian ghosts. They might has well have been Hari Karis for the minimal part they were to play in Patti's life. She looked strange accompanying two of them the mile or so along Fifth Avenue to their Shadyside dwelling on that hot June afternoon. It was a distorted view like heat rising from hot asphalt making straight lines wavy.

After a long shower and a short meal she felt a bit better Her two new companions suggested she take a nap which she did after secreting her seed stash deep in the corner of the couch on which she lay.

Patti continued her way across the country and eventually found her true love of the times, ironically a descendant of her idol, Appleseed, but as these things often go, over time their marriage soured. Soon there was much bitterness between Patti Chapman and her husband. Apple seeds and pot seeds just didn't mix well.

Her husband being "born again" as a way out of his marital misery, became delusional and decided to rid the world of all evil, divorce the bitch, and gain revenge.

Not thinking clearly as he went through their record albums, he came across some recorded under the "Apple" label. "This was monstrous," he thought. These rock musicians were sacrilegious, desecrating the symbol of his ancestor. The drug induced musicians and their product needed to be erased. He was especially offended by a press release where one of the Apple group bragged that they were more popular that God.

The husband took out his God inspired revenge on both the marijuana and the apple fantasy that had inspired Patti. Misguidedly he took out his hatred on Apple records and one of his perceived drug proponents. Months later in New York City the descendant of Johnny (Appleseed) Chapman thinking of the purity of the Dakotas, fatally shot one of the members of the world's best known and most revered musical groups ever to be named after a bug.

Patti disappeared into an oblivion she could not have imagined. Years later their daughter became a congressional intern.

Soft Rock

Shannon, you were twenty months
old. On a short walk with your
mom, you picked up some stones.
You gave me one—it was the one
you liked best. I love it. It
with the first "thing" you gave
to me and means much. You've
given me joy and laughter too, and
they mean more, but I'll always
love that stone—and you.

Love,
Dad

Freudian Shadows

It had been a long time
      Since I'd seen you when
You weirdly appeared in my
      Bed last night.
It was your wedding day
      And your once fearful
Eyes were tearful as you stood
      Like a lovely statue angel at
The altar all alone.
      Yet, despite damp cheeks,
You still smiled.
      I always knew you
Didn't want to marry him.
      I smiled in my dream
For you.

Country Music Poem

You know it baby, and I do, too.
When it comes to us, as of late
Too many times we've both been blue.
Things just haven't been that great.
I'm no longer certain how much I care,
But I really don't want to separate.
I just wanna refinance this love affair
Because of the lower interest rate.

Splashdown

The idea was there
for a moment:
my mind jolted by
the flash.
But there was no need
at that second
to produce any more
of this trash.
The candle was lit,
but it flickered;
then went out
with a puff.
I guess I just
wasn't ready to
write any more
of this stuff.
Since it went out
in a hurry,
leaving not even
a spark,
You've wasted your time
in this reading, just to be left
in the dark.

To Marilyn (1926-1962)

You were pretty beyond my comprehension,
      Miss Monroe, and enticing to a
young lad, but distant from my age, dreams,
      experience, or grasp. Now, twenty-five
years later, I look at your films and
      news clips, and you have found eternity.
Now you're even younger than I. Whatever,
      I hope you're content. You aren't
an actress anymore; you are real now.

Mirror Memory

The Morning mirror
remembered last night when
in complete blackness,
I was shaving my face
but the razor was a
glittering gold Rolex
wristwatch. The metallic
band crawled like tank
treads over my cheek
knocking down whiskers I
couldn't see in my sleep.

Hey, Barbara!

Hey, Barb—
    The first time I ever
    had an Arby's Roast
    Beef was in Pittsburgh
    with you.
    The first time I ever
    had lobster tail was
    in Pittsburgh with you.
    What does this mean?

Devon Prep School

I teach at Devon Prep.
It's one of those schools
where the majority
of students come from
families who have whitewall
tires on their gas grills.

Waterfall

Billions of bubbling
drops congealed as one body
like the souls of humanity
flowing endlessly in time.

The Talisman

The talisman appeared forty eight years ago. Whether it brought good fortune or ill I suppose I'll never know, but that fateful day has certainly affected the course of my life and subsequently the lives of many others.

Almost nine years old, I lived in a very small town roughly one hundred miles from my birthplace, Philadelphia, where I had been born breech birth on Labor Day in an elevator in Temple University Hospital. My mom didn't recall the travel direction of the elevator but often teased that she was going to name me "Otis" after its inventor. Instead, she named me after the intern who delivered me.

Beautiful and remote, the Pennsylvania coal region was refreshing compared to my vague memories of the grayness of Philadelphia. Woodlands abounded. Mountain streams and wildlife were well within a nine-year-old's walking distance.

I lived in a large rented house in Frackville with my family. My grandparents and my uncle always went out of their way to entertain me. My dad worked in a strip mine with my uncle and grandfather. Mom was pretty busy working in a nearby department store. I'm not too sure how my older brother spent his time, but I remember the day when my half-wacko grandmother chased him with a butcher knife. It was kind of funny because she was about eighty-five and couldn't have caught a turtle. After that incident she was placed in a nursing home.

My many good friends and I had Huck Finn like adventures and general good times. Movie matinees cost nine cents, comic books ten, a fountain coke at Sheridan's drug store was only a nickel, and household doors were not locked at night. It was really the best of times.

Then, the worst happened. My mom grew ill and needed to be closer to the much better medical facilities in Philly. In dire financial condition, the ecology effecting strip mines were also going under. In order to achieve financial stability my rough exteriored dad decided we should retreat to the more prosperous environs of suburban Philadelphia.

When the news struck me in the middle of an excellent, adventurous summer, it hit very hard. Leaving Jimmy Campbell, Larry Moore, Ray and George Lord and my childhood sweetheart Caroline Galba was a devastating thought, further complicated by the reality that I would be isolated with my older brother until I formed new friendships in what I knew was to be an alien world.

Always imaginative, probably because of my reading, I was plagued with terrifying mental conjurations. I was being forced from Eden into Hell despite being innocent of any damning sins. The story of the country mouse and the city mouse had years before colored my thoughts on city life. Canoeing dressed as Indians and shooting rubber tipped arrows at each other would cease. Fun would die.

Not able to face the rapidly approaching reality, I retreated into my books. I rapidly devoured an edition of *Treasure Island*, the one with the wonderful N.C. Wyeth illustrations. I can still picture the images of Blind Pew, and the one with Jim Hawkins threatening, "One more step Mr. Hands, and I'll blow your brains out." Ironically, I now live only a few minutes from the studio where Wyeth plied his trade and where his equally famous son, Andrew, now an old man, continues to utilize the family gift.

At any rate, *Treasure Island* got my pre-adolescent mind into a pirate mode. Getting into what today would be called "action figures" I got my mom to purchase a rubber-plastic compound primitive by today's standards.

A week or so before the dreaded move, I had a strange compulsion. The pirates were bland, unconvincing, of no character. I took the more malicious of the two, obviously the captain because of the skull and crossbones on his hat and the cutlass in his hand, and cut off his leg. I drove a nail into the stump to effect a peg leg. Still not satisfied, I got rid of the beige with various colors of model airplane paint. Black, yellow, and red gave him life like a Wyeth pirate before I set him aside to dry.

I've no idea why, but within a week of the dreaded move, I decided to send my pirate on his own journey. Fashioning a raft from a few pieces of wood, wire, popsicle sticks, and glue, I fastened the buccaneer to a primitive mast with glue and a jewelry chain. A few blocks from our house, I placed the raft into a small creek. With tears flowing, I pushed him into his proportional sea, and returned home.

About a week later we moved from placid Frackville to the noisy, busy, suburban hell of Brookhaven. I hated it. I hated the citified type kids, I hated the school, I hated the teachers, I hated my older brother who couldn't replace my friends, and I even hated my parents for doing this to me.

Somehow, my father, who was rarely sensitive to anything, sensed my state. When I was several weeks into my acute depression, he decided to spend a few rare moments with his youngest son. He took me fishing, not that I derived any pleasure from it, to a place called Fortescue, New Jersey, close to the fluid juncture of the Delaware River and Delaware Bay.

Walking miserably along the beach while my dad was fishing, I reflected. Even this place was terrible. Salt water was not fresh water; the air had a smell to it. It wasn't clean. And what was this dirty sand? I hated sand, and I still do. As I continued my self-pitying walk, I suddenly saw something colorful in the sand ahead. I stared in disbelief. Bending down, I picked up my painted peg-legged pirate from the beach. My pirate had journeyed at least one hundred thirty miles from a small mountain creek to the Schuylkill River into the Delaware River to the edge of the bay. I smiled in elated disbelief. The paint job was still good, and the peg leg nail actually looked better with its accumulated rust. I intensely stared and reflected for a moment and then threw the damn thing back into the water.

Somehow that moment foreshadowed the rest of my life.

Doritos

I'm addicted to them,
but I don't like them.
The only thing good about
them is you can't tell if
they're stale unless you're
Mexican.

American Poetry

Even the best can be improved.
"Two paths" diverged in a yellow
wood would have been better
unless Frost was traveling by
car.

Ode to Tycho Brahe (1546-1601)

It's very sad that fewer than
1% of the western population of
this late great planet Earth at
the end of the 20th century know
that you had a real Renaissance
nose for science and gave up your
sense for the advancement of mankind!
But, maybe, the lesson to be learned
is to keep your proboscis out of
other people's business.

The Epitome of Conceit

The ultimate stuffed shirt
would have to be Jeremy Bentham.

Serious Sunburst

Intellect driven, Shannon
chases life like a huntress
her prey, beaming beauty
sunbursts through thunderous
electrified skies searching
for sense in an inane world
finally evoking a captivating,
peaceful smile.

Willowy Wonder

Almost constant sunshine,
Amber scatters clouds
with her mind, beauty and wonder.
Creative humor displayed with
compassion and loyalty, she glows
through the days with puppy
playfulness and wisdom developed
into the strength of gentleness
from patient kindness with smiles.

The Disillusionment of Being
Disillusioned in Florida

The paradoxical fallacy is
simply the obverse of the illogicality
of the statement. In other words, although
it's still true, who cares?

Jerry's Poem

Sometimes life bounces
    you around a bit.
Kind of like being hit
    by a baseball bat.
This time instead of a
strike three batter
You are once again the ball,
        but you're been fielded
By the right hand. This
    time, my friend and
None too soon—You're caught!

To Bad, Baby

I was hardly even looking
When I saw your eyes see mine.
Something inside you was cooking
As though intoxicated with wine.
I tried to look away—but I couldn't—
Your beauty too magic like fire.
I wanted to talk, but I wouldn't...
Still I can't deny the desire.
Sadly shy—was little I could do.
Time continues, and I'll never see you
This event was not the everyday kind.
Your image is forever etched in my mind.

Icy Sheet

What is this ice?
       It's only September.
Some ice is nice, like when
       it covers a lake, and with
       skates on, you can glide and
       soar freely.
Icicles are nice, too. They're pretty!
Ice cubes serve something soothing.
Icing on pastry provides pleasure.
       But this enveloping sheet is
       like the ice that
       coats windshields.
It's hard, coldcrusty, and cuts
       and you can't see through it.
It's dangerous and somehow needs
       rapid defrosting so
we can clearly see each other
       again.
I don't know about you,
       but
       it gives me chills, makes me shiver.
Hugs are warm.

Static Cling

I want us to roll around in a
big commercial dryer making
love, with the heat off, of
course—no need for that.

When the cycle is over, I'd like
us to exit through the port hole,
cling free and static free. Would
more "Bounce" help?

Books and Their Covers

More than they tell
    Book covers hide...
        Like clothing, covering
            The nakedness of
                The ideas inside.

Clock Faces

Clock faces can be
pleasant or not. It
depends on what's in
your mind. Observing
the positions of the
hands, they can seem
like pliers pinching the
seconds, or like scissors
snipping away at eternity.

Smiles

It's only natural
        for a smile
to beget its own kind,
smiles being infectious
        like yawns.
            Be careful
though. Smiles can
be wrongly seen. Beware
of returning one to
someone who smiles
        when angry.

The Benevolence of Milton S. Hershey

There have been many Miltons, as in
Berle, John, and Hershey who gave
immeasurable joy, but my mind salivates
picturing the dark chocolate squares
divided into easily breakable bits of
delight. Then, of course, there was the alternative
unpatterned bar doused with random almonds,
Ah, Mr. Hershey, you were a real life
Willie Wonka.

:

Blood, Dog Poop, and Puppy Love

"C'mon, Georgie, You don't have to go to school," I ployed.

"I'll get hided if I skip Kindergarten again," he moaned.

"But if you get on that bus, I'll be alone all morning. I won't have anybody to play cowboys with, and I just got my new Colt six-shooter like yours," I responded.

Georgie King was this bad little kid from up the street. His family was tough. His dad had just gotten out of jail, and his oldest brother, then about fifteen, was always in trouble. He had a real pretty sister though, who was smart and in college. I think she became a Miss Pennsylvania. There was also another brother, Ray, about seven, who was a friend of mine too.

"Georgie, if you don't hide from that bus, we're not going to be blood brothers anymore."

"Jimmy, I told you, I'll really get in trouble."

"So what! You're always telling me how you're so brave and tough. Prove it."

"Ah, okay Jimmy, you win. You always do, but I know I'm gonna get spanked."

"Why don't we get Ray to play with us too? He hates school."

"That's a good idea. Then if we get caught, my mom will have to be mad at both of us. She won't be so hard on me."

"Great, let's go."

It was easy to convince Ray. We hid out in the foundation of this old house they were knocking down across the street from where I lived. As the school bus went by, we giggled. It was a beautiful day in September on the top of the mountain, and the three of us would have it all to ourselves. Another adventure.

Since my mom was on her way to work, I went into the house and swiped some chocolate cookies my grandmom had baked (enough for the three of us) while Georgie and Ray hid across the street.

Soon we were hiking down the mountain to Pottsy Hollow, about two miles away. We had our cap pistols and I had my red cowboy hat on. We were ready. Let the Apaches try to ambush us. They'd be dead sorry.

"Jimmy, how come you don't go to Kindergarten like Georgie? You're the same age," asked Ray.

"Oh, I'm lucky. My mom says I already know everything they teach in Kindergarten so it would be a waste of time. I'm going to just start first grade next year." I replied.

"Man, you're lucky," they echoed together.

I started thinking about something then. I guess it was an elementary approach, considering my age, but it must have been my first inclination of a trait that was to profoundly affect the rest of my life, and not always in a good way, either.

Tramping through the woods, I kept looking at Ray and Georgie. Georgie was my age but bigger and stronger. Ray was two years older and much tougher. Yet it was a fact; I was the leader. They were like marionettes, just like my Howdy Doody puppet. I pulled the strings, and they never resisted. I could convince them to do anything. Suddenly, I didn't like them anymore. I guess I thought they were boring or something. Clearly superior, I didn't want to play with them anymore, but we were all the way down the hollow, and we had our guns and all, and I knew there were Apaches all around. I couldn't quit, but I was bored.

"Hey, Ray," I asked, Know how the Indians proved they were brave?"

"No, how, Jimmy?"

"They let their friends take target practice at them."

"Nuh."

"Yes, they did too. Honest. I read about it in a comic book called *The Deerslayer*."

"Well, what about it?"

"Let's have a bravery contest," I suggested.

"How... What do you mean?" asked Georgie.

"Well, especially you and Ray. You're always talking about how tough you are. Let's see if you can pass the Indian test."

"That's dumb. You can't be a target for cap pistols. They're not real," quipped Ray.

"No, you're right, but you can be a target for this old hunting knife my uncle gave me."

"You're nuts," Ray challenged.

"No, I'm not, but you're a coward and not brave at all," I retorted.

I had all the confidence in the world. I could have been a circus knife thrower at the age of five and a half. For real, with all my spare time practicing instead of going to school I could toss that thing and hit within an inch or so and make it stick, too. Somehow, it all had to do with wrist action and the feeling when you held the blade.

"Hey, Ray, you sissy, I'll do it," Georgie responded.

Well we stood him up against this fat old tree with smooth bark. I lined up about five feet in front of him.

"Okay, now don't blink, Georgie. You're not allowed to blink, or you're not brave, and don't move 'cause you don't know where I'm aiming and you could move into the knife."

Swish! Thud! The knife stuck about four inches to the left of his left ear.

"Great Georgie! Now let's see if Ray is as brave."

"Oh, all right," Ray reluctantly agreed.

"Okay, Ray," I said, as I pulled the knife from the tree.

Swish! Thud! The knife left my hand and ended up close to the same spot. No! It was closer. About four inches closer. The blood trickled down from Ray's ear. For a few seconds he just stood there.

"Jimmy, you son of a bitch, I'm going to kill you," he snarled.

As he yanked the knife from the tree, I could see that it had nicked his ear ever so slightly, just enough to make it bleed. Even so, I didn't stick around. I sped through the woods with the King brothers chasing me, whooping like Indians whose totem pole had just been destroyed.

Running for what seemed like forever, with unknown fear behind me, I was still ahead of them as I turned to corner the safety of my house. Putting on a final burst of speed, I tripped over a tree branch on the grass and fell head first in to a huge pile of fresh dog poop. Its donator must have been sick, too. I was a mess. It was all over me, and the King brothers had caught up to me. They didn't hurt me though. They just stood there howling at me. Finally, they turned and walked away, hands on their stomachs to keep them from bursting with glee. Nature sure has a strange way of protecting people sometimes.

Needless to say, my friendship with Georgie and Ray was finished, but the next afternoon while walking up the back alley, I met the cutest girl playing on a new backyard swingset. She had just moved in. We became super good friends - for a while. Strangely enough, her name was Georgeanne.

Waiting for the Light to Change

Lonestar on the radio
      with "Tequila Talking,"
And when it comes to us
      I'll be walking
My head is clouded: my thoughts
      are fuzzy
I can't think at all, and
      it's 'cause we
Just don't get along anymore.
I'm waiting for the light to change.

Political Appointees

The ideal position is to be
the Postmaster General.
Just think: You have
control of whose faces
adorn postage stamps, you
get paid very well, and you
get to supervise all the
workers stamping your approval
on all of those rural mail
box doors. What a job!

Just Another Bumper Sticker

Just one more bumper sticker:
"I break for people who can't spell."

Acid Rain

I read in the paper
the other day of an
experiment. Missiles
were to be fired, seeding
the clouds with barium.
The expected result was
clouds of green, purple,
and bright blue. It
made me Leary thinking
of the colored raindrops
if there were a storm.

Vanity

It's a riot. Observing
    daily the constant
        primping
of adolescents, it
seems that, upon, pubescence
    each should be
    presented with a
    portable, full-length
    mirror.

Guilty

When you commit a crime, it's
        important not to leave any evidence.
So please, since I haven't committed
        a capital offense, when you're
        finished reading this, please
        burn this poem.
My theft of your time is at least
        a misdemeanor.

Just Once More (please)

Just once more I have to see you.
One last time will be enough.
Because you're ugly through and through
And my stomach's not that tough.

Staplers

Staplers seem such
a cruel tool for fastening
things together—especially
fragile papers. To be
pierced twice when once
would suffice. It seems
that a paper clip or
even glue binding would
be more gentle and humane.

Ode to Age

I've never been much concerned
with age.
But lately it's had me in a
rage.
It steals upon you like an
enemy,
And attacks, leaving no remedy.
The body's vitals begin to
decline,
First with the physical, then
with the mind.
Most I can take, I don't really
care,
But Age, please at least—
leave me my hair!

Nocturnal

Talking on the telephone,
I really wanted it to
be something.
    We said all we
could to each other
and then, that
damned silence.

Geriatric Lycanthropy

Feeling my way through a dream last night,
I found myself near dawn on a park bench.
Soon I heard sobbing, and as I strained
to hear, an old forlorn figure approached.
As he drew nearer and sat next to me, the
tragedy was obvious. He was a senior citizen
werewolf.

"What's the matter, pal?" I asked.
"Can I help?"

"Thanks, but no," sobbed the gray furry
canine. "It's my dentures. I can't even make
a good bite anymore. Everyone just laughs.
I can't scare anymore."

"Have you tried Fasteeth?" I asked.
"No," he responded. "I'm at my wit's
end. I'd welcome a silver bullet. Besides,
there are too many real terrorists in the
world today."

I didn't know what to say, so I arose
with tears in my eyes.

"I wish I could help," I said. "Good
luck buddy."

His truth overwhelmed me.

Sunburn

I watched her browning
    in the sun
    for a long time.
She occasionally flipped
    over to make sure
the sunoven rays
    were evenwarming.
When she was well done,
    I gobbled her up
    into my life.

Abe Lincoln in Chadds Ford

(for Rea Redifer)

Abe's spirit moves miles through time
from Gettysburg to the Brandywine
conveyed by mind, brush and paint.
then elevated to the status of saint
by the artist who really knows him best
whose portraits differ from those of the rest.
Not just the details down to the mole
His colors breathe life into his soul.
The life's work of this mystic sleuth
is unmasking myth to reveal the truth.
He plies his craft with his water dyes
Until the spirit glows again in Abe's eyes.
There are just those times when he gets to thinkin'
that he's got to paint another Abe Lincoln.
The life giving brush brings death to the sword
And Abraham Lincoln still lives in Chadds Ford.

Singular Sob Story

I looked at her
toothbrush holder on the wall.
Six slots but had only one brush. I
wondered—had there been others
who moved away, or had it always
been there, mostly in the dark, alone,
without companions? Upon a
second glance, I saw the dry bristles,
yet the handle dripped tears. It
made me sad.

Dumbo

Barb and I were strolling the boardwalk
    in Wildwood, N.J.
Awful as it was, a seagull
    d
    r
    o
    p
    p
    e
    d
        on her hair.
I assured her that it was a sign
    of good luck, followed with
"Be thankful elephants don't fly."
I rethought, "Damn, she would be
    the luckiest girl in the world?"

.

Self-Knowledge

I just thought of something which
disturbs me appreciably.
I never have, nor will I ever be
able, to first-handedly know what
I look like with my eyes closed.

In No Sense

Do you remember, can you recall
One of those happiest days of all?
You looked at her; she was so sweet
As you blindly walked down that street.
The world came alive, and it was just grand
The day you first managed to hold her hand.
But then it all started, as these things do.
You see, I know, because I once was you.
The relationship grew, as we tend to say.
But as is always, it didn't stay that way.
It got more involved, and flesh touched flesh.
Eventually the feelings were no longer fresh.
So listen to this, young ladies and gents.
It's best to hold on to your innocence.

Christmas Overkill

Go out and get your tree.
      Be sure it still has life.
Nice and green—no dry needles.
      Take it from its cold home,
And place it by the suffocating
      Fireplace inferno.
Remember to cut a slice from
      The bottom of the trunk,
So it can drink from the wound
When you don't forget to water it.
Or is it just that it's too much trouble
      To get down on your knees and
Get needles in your hair?
      Then, best of all, while it sits
Bleeding sap into the water,
      Go get the lights and
Plug them in to be sure they fire.
      Now, yes, send that voltage
Through the branches. Zap it
      As a reward for its beauty!

Old Songs (late '50s, '60s, etc.)

Old songs revolving
      at 45 per minute
      drum their way
          into my brain through
    my ears.
The vibrations continue
         d

            o

                w

                    n
            through my body
        to my feet as I
      take you out on the
        dance floor
            for another spin in
            perfect time.

The Flirt

I was only teasing you,
　　　At least I was at first.
Knowing I was pleasing you
　　　Only made it worse.
Innocent intentions then began to fade
　　　Overcome by lustful thought.
Fed by many compliments you paid,
　　　Then I knew I had you caught.
Hidden excitement behind my smile,
　　　You still were not aware.
Another conquest made with style.
　　　But I wasn't being fair.
I don't know why it's such fun
　　　To lead on and entice.
It was just another hit and run;
　　　Another roll of the dice.
It's a curse to have such fate;
　　　To never fail or be shot down.
Then, my dear, it was getting late.
　　　You were left with just a frown.
It's a bitch, I'll have you know.
　　　Still, I have to feed my ego.

Stupid Poem

I just can't believe
      your stupidity.
You're so damned dumb,
      I'm surprised you even
      know how to
         breathe.

The Party's Over

It was as clear as ice.
The sky divided into multi-
Colored sections though it was night,
Like an illuminated earth globe
With tinted national territories.
Despite the dream silence, the
Noise deafened the ears. Then
It began—spherical lights of
Incredible size—first there—
Then here—speeding beyond
Sight measure. Below we watched
Speechless as the lasers sought
And found and destroyed the Heavens.
The blackened burning sky opened
To admit purple, and it was over.

Shyster

Beware of the
      accountant whose
Rubber dullness is
      displayed by his
Brand new #2 pencil
      perfectly pointed but
With a worn-down eraser.

Abused

I was getting to the breaking point;
        tired of being battered and bruised.
One broken nose, two fractured fingers,
        cracked ribs, numerous contusions and
        black eyes later,
            I'd simply had it.
I cringed as the front door opened.
Would my spouse be a holy terror again?

Not to take chances,
        I threw on my jacket, pushed my
      way through the door, and yelled back,
"Betty, it's over. I'm leaving you
               forever."

The Squirrel

Tonight while driving home
I inadvertently hit a squirrel.
Remorsefully, I stopped.
Picking him up, I saw he
Wasn't dead.
He tried to bite—I wouldn't allow.
Placing him gently on the side of the
Road with red hands, he looked
At me with rodent hatred in
His eyes, and then he slept forever,
But I bled, too.

Deception

Lately you've become
a lie—so many-faced
that you're like an
actress, who, after
so many films has
forgotten which role
is the real her. At
that rate, whatever part
is played, the feature
is bound to be
          a tragedy.

An Addition to Oz

Somewhere there exists a
world so beautiful that,
despite the warmth, the
rocks and trees and eaves
are decorated forever
with icicles in prismatic
colors. I want to find it.

The Fast Break

I had planned the job for two months. Two months of constant thought, careful observation. Two months of suddenly awakening from troubled sleep to jot down another idea, another possibility. Finally, the details seemed solidified. Every angle was covered. Even with the hour rapidly approaching, I was totally confident.

Of course, time is always a factor when you're trying to pull off a heist. I knew my own capabilities. Nothing could go wrong.

I met Rhonda down at Dolan's Pub, just two blocks from the Savings and Loan. We sat, had a few drinks, and quietly and cautiously went over the details one final time.

As the time was approaching, we went out to my new Porsche, which I had purchased a few weeks beforehand. Chosen for its speed and handling, I knew it wouldn't fail to extricate us from the scene in a flash. All Rhonda had to do was keep it running and keep her blue eyes open for a few minutes while I went inside.

It was all too easy. All I had to do was use the key and turn the combination and I was in the safe. Three minutes loading up the two sacks and I'd be a million and a half dollars richer. Twenty-three seconds from the vault to the awaiting car, four minutes and eleven seconds from the Savings and Loan to the dock. One half-minute more to the boat—then into the darkness of the bay and home free.

I envisioned myself and Rhonda, too, living in tropical luxury as we had dreamed. Sure, they would figure out that she had given me the key so I could make an impression. They'd know that she told me the combination as well, but by the time they even realized it, we'd be well on our way through the night. I also knew there was no extradition from Grand Cayman. We'd be safe.

Before I knew it, I was in the vault, the money sacks were stuffed. I threw them over my shoulder and headed for the landing. Oh damn! That hurt. My knee ached like hell. I had slipped on the stairs. I couldn't stand up. It must be dislocated. Clutching onto the bags desperately, I pulled myself erect. Dragging my left leg, I got to the door, but time was out of sync now. I had to hurry. I knew the cops had heard the alarm and were on their way by now.

As I threw the bags in the purring Porsche and flung myself in the passenger seat I said, "C'mon, Rhonda baby. Let's get the hell out of here."

She said, "What happened? Hurry up, get over here!"

"No," I said. "You drive, baby. Let's go!"

"Oh hell," she cried. "Don't you remember, I told you once that I can't drive a stick shift?"

The next sound I heard were the sirens as three squad cars corralled us. I guess I didn't think of everything.